Management Guide to Handling Stress

Kate Keenan

RAVETTE PUBLISHING

Published by Ravette Publishing Limited
P.O. Box 296
Horsham
West Sussex RH13 8FH

Telephone: (01403) 711443
Fax: (01403) 711554

Series Editor – Anne Tauté
Editor – Catriona Scott

Cover design – Jim Wire
Printing & Binding – Cox & Wyman Ltd.
Production – Oval Projects Ltd.

An Oval Project
produced for Ravette Publishing.

Cover – Undoing the knot of stress
is easier than you think. All it takes
is a bit of an effort.

Acknowledgement:
Angela Summerfield

Contents

This book is dedicated to
those who would like to manage better
but are too busy to begin.

Handling Stress

Everyone is under stress. But not all stress is the kind that impairs your performance. If it was, there would be no mountaineers or deep-sea divers – people who thrive on stress. The important difference is that they can handle the stress, because they take control of the circumstances in which they experience it.

In everyday life, stress usually takes the form of mental or physical tension which you would rather not have. At work, it generally boils down to the pressures to get things done. It is when these forces become too great that people feel out of control, and generally are. This is because stress affects your ability to think clearly and clouds your judgement.

It will help to stop pressure from becoming too stressful if you can recognize the symptoms of stress and take preventative action. Fortunately it is never too late to start.

This book helps you understand how stress could be affecting your life and offers ways to handle it.

★ ★ ★ ★ ★

1. The Need to Handle Stress

Stress is the reaction people have to excessive pressure. The rapid pace of life today and everyone's increased expectations mean that people have to tolerate more pressure now than ever before. They get used to living with stress, and strive to meet ever-increasing amounts while wondering why they do not seem able to get the pleasure out of life that they once did. More often than not this is because they fail to realize that stress needs to be handled.

Sorting Good Stress from Bad

For most people the term 'stress' has negative associations. But in fact there are two kinds:

1. **Good Stress** (or 'eu-stress'). To get the most out of life everyone needs some 'good stress' to act as an impetus to meet challenges. The technical term for stress is 'arousal'. You need to be sufficiently aroused to get out of bed and go to work. As the day goes on, you become more alert until you reach your optimum performance, which is when you do your best work.

2. **Bad Stress** (or 'dys-stress'). This results in feeling that the pressures in your life have become over-

6

whelming and you are no longer able to cope. It is the type of stress that people really mean when they say they are 'stressed'. If left unresolved, bad stress can escalate from a feeling of being snowed under to becoming physically ill.

Whether good stress becomes bad stress will very much depend on individual circumstances and personal strength. The onset of 'dys-stress' can be sudden, prompted by a specific incident. But for many people it is cumulative, as skills for coping gradually degenerate and the ability to function declines. This need not be an inexorable process: if you can recognize early signs of stress, you can begin to do something to counteract its effects.

Recognizing Signs of Stress

The clue to whether someone is succumbing to stress is a change in behaviour. The most common signs are:

- Getting ratty with people and over-reacting at the least problem.

- Having less energy than usual and so achieving less.

- Being more argumentative and quibbling about things which would normally be acceptable.

- Needing a drink to get going.

- Feeling persistently miserable and gloomy.

- Having a sense of being out of control: of being swamped by demands – all of which need to be addressed and coped with at the same time.

- Experiencing unwelcome physical reactions such as a racing heart, a churning stomach, sweating, shivering, headaches and skin rashes.

It is easy to think these responses may be due to life just being more difficult than it used to be, or that because circumstances are constantly changing it is impossible to keep pace with events so there is not much point in even trying. In fact, such reasoning is symptomatic of someone working under stress.

Adopting Negative Strategies

When people are stressed, they generally adopt strategies to alleviate their discomfort. Unfortunately, these are more often negative than positive.

Typical strategies are:

- **Running away**: ignoring a problem or pretending that there is no problem; denying that anything is wrong and declaring when asked that everything is alright, although it is obvious to everyone else that everything is not.

- **Fretting**: brooding over your worries and their consequences without taking any action to change them.

- **Vacillating**: dithering between one decision and another in order to avoid committing yourself to a definite course of action.

- **Procrastinating**: diverting energies from the job in hand by engaging in delaying tactics, doing anything rather than making a start.

- **Seeking excitement**: doing reckless things as a distraction from feeling dispirited.

- **Venting emotions**: erupting in anger, stinging remarks, or tears as a release for feelings of exasperation, agitation and disquiet.

- **Becoming a couch-potato**: withdrawing from taking part in activities which formerly would have been of interest.

All these strategies involve people doing things which are not only unproductive but which can make them feel more stressed in the long run. They are an unconscious attempt to get rid of pent-up feelings but, in reality, they simply create further stress.

Summary: Focussing on Stress

People tend to experience stress when the pressures around them become excessive. However, they are not always aware that the discomfort they are feeling is stress. Nor do they realize that if they could correctly identify the signs, they could do something about it.

One of the manifestations of stress is that people often adopt totally inappropriate ways of dealing with it. The methods they choose frequently precipitate more stress rather than reduce it.

Not all stress is debilitating. Good stress activates mechanisms which help people to cope with challenging circumstances. But bad stress is an insidious condition which requires to be understood if it is to be handled positively.

Questions to Ask Yourself

Think about your attitude to stress and how you usually react to it, and answer the following questions:

- Have I recently found myself over-reacting to fairly trivial things?

- Do I find it difficult to make even the most simple decision?

- Do I seem to be always tired for no discernable reason?

- Do I think I have too much to cope with?

- Do I tend to ignore problems in the hope that they will go away?

- Do I delay facing up to an issue?

- Am I incessantly turning things over and over in my mind with no conclusion?

If you have answered 'Yes' to many or all of these questions, you are showing typical signs of 'dys-stress' and need to do something about it.

You Will Be Doing Better If...

★ You appreciate that there is a difference between good stress and bad stress.

★ You acknowledge that bad stress is a reaction to excessive pressure.

★ You are able to recognize that lack of energy, putting things off, introspection, irritability and explosive behaviour are all signs of stress.

★ You are aware that adopting negative strategies is not an effective way to handle stress.

★ You recognize that pretending problems do not exist will not make stress disappear.

★ You realize that not handling stress makes you more stressed than ever.

2.   Understanding Stress

Understanding the nature of stress is the first step in the process of handling it.

The Stress Response

The physical reaction to stress has been programmed in human beings from prehistoric times. It is a basic survival instinct which involves a complex sequence of responses to a 'perceived' threat.

When stone-age man came face to face with a hairy mammoth, his brain signalled fright and prepared his body to deal with the emergency by mobilising it for two courses of action:

- **Fight** – confronting the aggressor.

- **Flight** – running away as fast as possible.

The threats which people face in modern life may not be the same, but the response is.

Battle Stations in the Body

When the brain interprets a situation as alarming, the hypothalmus – the 'stress centre' in the brain – triggers a number of simultaneous processes in the body, as if readying it for battle, as follows:

1. The **sympathetic nervous system** releases adrenaline into the blood stream. This increases the heart rate and blood pressure – two things which stimulate the state of arousal required to provide a quick energy fix so that you are prepared for action. The problem is that the process drains the blood from the brain and therefore the oxygen supply. As oxygen is needed by the brain to function rationally, this explains why people can freeze or do something irrational in threatening situations.

2. The **endocrine system** releases the body's 'major stress hormone' (adrenocorticotrophic hormone – ACTH) which increases the glucose levels in the blood thus fuelling the muscles to respond to the emergency. This means that the body is fully primed to act and explains why people can do superhuman things when they are in danger.

All this activity is gearing the body to protect itself. The breathing rate increases, the body's natural painkillers (the endorphins) are activated, more red blood cells are released to help carry oxygen and more white corpuscles are produced to fight infection.

If the threat is of an immediate kind, such as a near-fatal accident, once you get out of danger the body begins the calming down process. As the reaction to the emergency subsides, the **parasympathetic system** (the one that restores energy) takes over and returns the body to its normal state.

But if the threat has been present for some time and involves prolonged tension (such as spending days preparing for a speech), the body will take much longer to come back to a balanced state once the event has taken place.

And if the threat is a constant menace so that your body's call to 'battle stations' is not able to let up – the kind of stress experienced in meeting endless and ever-increasing demands – the body is unable to relax or feel comfortable because the ACTH stress hormone is continuously being activated. It therefore never gets a chance to revert to a balanced state.

It is immediately apparent why, through persistent pressure, your defence system would stay on constant alert and could eventually fail you from sheer exhaustion.

Intense physiological arousal of this sort which extends over a very long period can ultimately be extremely harmful. Although the body begins to recover from the initial alarm-reaction, the blood glucose levels become dangerously low, thus depleting the body's resources and making it more susceptible to disorders such as heart disease, high blood pressure, asthma or even the common cold. Therefore, the earlier positive action is taken, the better.

Shell Shock to the Brain

Most modern-day situations which cause you stress are not so extreme that they require you to take the fight or flight option. In any case, neither action would be appropriate.

The problem is that the brain cannot tell the difference between a serious life-threatening circumstance such as facing up to a hairy mammoth, or an unwelcome disturbance such as a personality clash at work. Regardless of the cause, the age-old stress response to what the mind interprets as a threat is set in motion. Within seconds adrenaline is charging round your system which, if not given a physical outlet, will produce a state of mental fluster accompanied by physical reactions such as churning sensations in the stomach, sweaty palms, pounding heart, dry mouth and weak limbs. Your body has instinctively primed itself for action, when what you need is a raised level of reasoning to temper that instinct.

Unfortunately all this physical disturbance has a dire effect on the thinking processes, the most common being:

- **Not being able to think straight**. You can find it hard to organize your thoughts logically so that you can tackle problems. Feeling frazzled often leads you to doubt your own competence.

- **Being easily distracted**. You can find it difficult to concentrate and as a result, your performance tends to deteriorate. A lack of concentration leads to difficulty in completing tasks.

- **Behaving in a more extreme way**. You can find yourself adhering rigidly to established patterns of behaviour. This leads to an incapacity to adapt when circumstances change and flexible responses are required.

The inability to think objectively about a situation makes it more difficult to cope in a constructive way. But once you realize the effect that stress can have on your reasoning, it is easier to take remedial action.

The Chain Reaction

Because your body and mind are inextricably linked, it is your initial appraisal of a situation which triggers the physical chain reaction and determines the intensity of the emotional response. If you interpret a certain situation as exciting and exhilarating (such as when an event is demanding, but manageable), the body's alarm system gives you the stimulus to take action. But if you interpret a situation as intimidating and upsetting (such as when work escalates and you are already at full stretch), a state of stress results.

Feelings do not arise out of the blue, they are a result of your perceptions. It is from your thoughts that your feelings and ultimately your behaviour arises. It follows, therefore, that if you allow your initial thoughts to start out as negative or 'faulty', you can easily feel jumpy, grumpy, miserable – all of which may cause you to behave in a stressed way.

Stressed feelings which remain unrelieved usually result in one or other of the following long-term conditions:

- **Anxiety**. When fears become unrealistic in relation to a situation, anxiety sets in. Symptoms include a sense of helplessness, feelings of panic, nervousness, jumpiness, and an inability to relax or to sleep.

- **Aggression**. When efforts to achieve a goal are frustrated, aggression results. Symptoms include extreme irritability, over-reaction to trivial things, and quarrelsome and bullying behaviour.

- **Depression**. When worries get out of proportion, life does not appear to hold many attractions, and depression takes hold. Symptoms include a loss of purpose, feelings of lethargy, weariness, weepiness and a sense of worthlessness.

These are the common consequences if stress is experienced over a period of time and, if nothing is done about it, these reactions get progressively worse.

Before such disquietudes become a way of life you need to identify the sources of stress which may be causing your lack of mental equilibrium.

Summary: Automatic Responses

Because the brain still responds to threat in the same way as it did when stone-age man walked the earth, you need to be aware of your own emotional responses to any given situation. It is your interpretation of whether or not something is threatening which determines the degree to which you feel stressed.

These atavistic responses are still as primitive as they were when human beings were hunter-gatherers. You would have thought that it would have evolved between the iron age and the age of the internet – but this is not the case. Modern man is not well-adapted to modern life. Once you understand the nature of stress you can see why.

Questions to Ask Yourself

Think about how you consider stress and ask yourself the following questions:

■ Do I understand that the purpose of the 'fight or flight' response is to maximize survival?

■ Do I appreciate that when the brain senses there is risk it gears the body to protect itself?

■ Am I aware that stress can prevent people from thinking straight?

■ Do I understand that prolonged stress depletes the body's resources, making it more susceptible to illness?

■ Do I recognize that prolonged stress may result in anxiety and/or depression?

■ Do I realize that it is how a situation is interpreted that triggers the body's alarm system?

You Will Be Doing Better If...

★ You appreciate that the brain still responds to stress in the same way as it did in prehistoric times.

★ You realize that the body activates defence mechanisms to protect itself when it feels threatened.

★ You understand that the body cannot return to a balanced state while the mind is on 'red alert'.

★ You are aware that a long-term background fear is more difficult to recover from than a far more frightening experience which is over quickly.

★ You understand that continuous feelings of stress can result in anxiety, aggression and depression.

★ You appreciate that thought processes can be impaired by stress.

★ You realize it is how you perceive a situation that determines how you react to it.

3. Pinpointing Your Stressors

When people are feeling stressed, they rarely take the time to think about why. Being able to put your finger on what is causing you stress (the stressor) enables you to deal with it more successfully because you will recognize that the stressor is rarely your fault.

In general, stressors derive from:

- **Your Own Intrinsic Drivers**. These are the innate compulsive forces which motivate people to push themselves in certain ways, sometimes to excess.

- **Workplace Pressures**. These are the requirements for people to carry out their tasks in situations where constraints and demands can conspire to prevent optimum performance.

- **Life Events**. These are the occasions – such as bereavement, divorce, debt or changing circumstances – which can push people to the limits of their capabilities and can sometimes cause them to re-evaluate how they manage their lives.

Intrinsic Drivers

Compulsive driving forces motivate your working style and affect everything you do. The way work is organized, time is managed, or personal relations are conducted are all subject to these drivers.

When you are not under stress they can be highly effective. But when you are stressed, they can drive your behaviour to extremes.

There are five basic drivers which compel people in their working lives:

- **Urgency**. With this driver, you are compelled to get a lot done in a short time. You also respond particularly well to short deadlines and your energy peaks under pressure. When not under stress, your strength is that you can achieve an enormous amount of work. But when stressed, all these characteristics become exaggerated, so you prepare less and more mistakes are made.

- **Perfection**. This driver compels you to achieve perfection, demanding that exacting standards be met. But under stress, you end up not trusting anyone to do things as well as you do and you inevitably become swamped with work. You are also likely to misjudge what is required and spend time unnecessarily being absorbed by more and more detail.

- **Pleasing people**. With this driver you aim to please without being asked and try to anticipate people's needs by working out what would be required and providing it. But under stress you may over-anticipate and inadvertently antagonize, or become over-sensitive, or get upset if you feel you have failed in your attempts.

- **Trying hard**. This driver compels you to put enormous effort into a task in your efforts to achieve. You tackle things enthusiastically, and are prepared to take on all and sundry. But under stress you can take on too much, so that less and less is accomplished.

- **Being strong**. This is the driver that compels you to be strong at all times and feel motivated when you are required to cope. You are extremely good at dealing with stressful situations and are very useful to have around in a crisis. But under stress you will never ask for help and struggle on alone whatever the personal cost.

Most people acknowledge that they are motivated by more than one of these driving forces. There is not much you can do to change them since, by their very nature, they are part of your nature. But if you are aware of your personal drivers, you will be able to recognize from your own behaviour the point at which they are becoming exaggerated. You can then try to tone them down, in much the same way as you would turn down the volume of a radio that is too loud.

Workplace Pressures

Feeling continuously pressured at work without taking the time to analyse why can add hugely to that pressure. Most people accept that a certain amount of stress 'goes with the job', but being able to pinpoint the sources of work-related stress which are frequently accepted as natural, yet which are not, will go a long way towards handling them. The most common kinds of workplace pressures are:

- **Coping with impossible standards** which have been set within an unrealistic timescale. As soon as the demands made exceed the capabilities and resources available, excessive stress arises, e.g. if people are working long hours, or have too much to do in the time given or if the work is problematic.

- **Working in changing circumstances** which means that the unexpected becomes the normal. If you are unsure of your own area of responsibility or there is no clear picture of what is expected of you, feelings of apprehension and demotivation will result.

- **Experiencing job insecurity** which leaves you feeling unsure and fearful of what the future holds. This can produce severe anxiety which in turn reduces performance and produces mood swings from bravura to the depths of depression.

- **Working with a disagreeable person** which can mean that your own and other people's finer feelings are overridden. This will result in lowered performance and feelings of frustration and tension.

- **Coping with too much responsibility** which means the buck stops with you far too often. Pressure results in a difficulty with making decisions, and with concentration.

- **Having too heavy a workload** which may mean you have too much to do in the time allocated or that you are not very good at setting priorities. The resulting pressure may cause you to become erratic and frantic, which creates more work.

In most of these circumstances, people are reacting to pressures not of their own making. This leaves them feeling that they are less in control of what they have to do which leads to the stress spiral: a fall in standards, an increase in grievances, a heightened sense of failure and, inevitably, more stress.

Taking the time to appraise your working life as soon as you begin feeling unusually pressurized enables you to pinpoint the causes of the stress. The process of doing so provides relief because you will now have some idea of where it originates. It also means you will not be adding to your stress by thinking that, somehow, you are to blame.

Life Events

Encountering innumerable changes and difficulties, ups and downs, is so much a part of life that you may have accepted levels of stress which are, in fact, unacceptable, in the same way as a sailor adapts to the rolling deck of a ship. Because of this, you should try to identify the issues in your life which are causing you stress. Think about how much of your stress is due to:

- **Major events**. The death of a close relative, marital separation, personal injury or illness, are obviously stressful. But so are events that are not sad or painful, such as getting married or moving house, simply because you are required to make substantial personal adjustments in coming to terms with a new situation which, however desirable, will make a considerable impact and thus cause stress.

- **Day-to-day aggravations**. While you expect to be stressed when you experience a major event in your life, many of these will be got over in time. But the kind of aggravations you experience on a daily basis (like encountering a traffic jam or being interrupted when trying to concentrate) do not fade away. They occur incessantly. No sooner do you deal with one when another takes its place. This causes much more stress than you realize because constant demands are being made upon your inner resources.

- **Ageing**. Adapting to mental and physical changes at different ages is more demanding than one might think, and can be a source of stress, especially at the mid-life point when hormones reduce (in men from around the age of 35 onwards, and in women more rapidly from their late 40s for 5-10 years). This has a direct effect on your physical well-being and behaviour, including some loss of short-term memory and lower levels of energy.

All these stressors may appear to be part of life's rich tapestry, and therefore circumstances with which you feel you should be able to cope, but you need to realize that virtually any change in life requires you to adapt, and that this by itself can cause stress.

An Accumulation of Stressors

It is important not to underestimate the effect which an accumulation of stressors can have in undermining your ability to manage. It is not the magnitude of one stressor or another that does this, but the cumulative effect. If the stressors arrived one at a time, you could probably handle them quite easily. But having to deal with various stressors at the same time generates over-powering stress. By happening together, they constitute a barrage from which there seems to be no escape.

It may appear that initially you are coping reasonably well with a combination of demanding drivers, workplace pressures and stressful life-events. However, the amount of effort required to do this slowly depletes your energy banks and reduces resilience so that some time later changes may occur in your physical health which may even bring about an extreme form of mental stress known as 'burnout'.

Summary: Sources of Stress

Stress can come from many sources, whether external events not of your making, or internal drivers which are part of your personality.

Identifying individual compulsions can help you to be aware of the way you function and how this behaviour can become more pronounced when you are under stress. It is also helpful to realize that a conjunction of pressures in your life and work can build up – like lava in a volcano – to produce all-engulfing stress.

Once you have pinpointed the events and areas of your life which are causing you stress, you can take remedial action to reduce their potentially damaging effects.

Questions to Ask Yourself

Think about how drivers, workplace pressures and life events may affect the way you perform, and answer the following questions:

■ Can I identify which drivers tend to motivate my behaviour?

■ Can I diagnose when these drivers seem to be getting out of control?

■ Do I recognize the workplace pressures which are causing me stress?

■ Do I accept that major events which are pleasant can cause just as much stress as unpleasant events?

■ Do I realize that constant daily nuisances account for a great deal of stress?

■ Do I understand that an accumulation of stressors can create more stress than the individual stressors themselves?

You Will Be Doing Better If...

★ You resolve to appraise your life in order to pin-point the things that cause you stress.

★ You are aware of the drivers that govern your behaviour.

★ You can sense when your drivers may be going into overdrive.

★ You realize how certain pressures at work can lead to stressful behaviour.

★ You recognize that daily aggravations draw on your inner reserves.

★ You understand that positive events can be just as stressful as the ones which are difficult to bear.

★ You are aware that it is the cumulative effect of stressors, not necessarily very stressful in themselves, which can cause you to feel excessively stressed.

4. Reducing Stress (Instantly)

The good thing about stress is that you can do something about it straightaway. Whether you are encountering aggression at work or coping with problems which arise unexpectedly, you are rarely in a position either to hit out (fight), or to turn on your heels and run (flight). But even when it is a case of 'what cannot be cured must be endured', you can find many ways of releasing the chemicals so injurious to your system.

No matter how much stress has built up, there is always a way of reducing it. But remember, you do not want to lose all stress altogether or you might never get up in the morning.

Using Stress Busters

Simple physical movement is an excellent way to relieve or alleviate tension immediately. Here are three tried and tested remedies which can be done anywhere. Try to do them several times a day.

- **Dropping your shoulders**. Sit up straight, raise your shoulders, and then drop them. This relaxes the muscles which in physical terms means you are not able to take flight, and therefore convinces your body for a few seconds that you are not under threat.

- **Breathing deeply**. Put your feet flat on the floor, rest your hands in your lap, drop your shoulders, shut your eyes, and take a deep breath by inhaling through the nose to a slow count of four, and exhaling through the mouth to a slow count of four. This gets the oxygen into the bloodstream via the lungs and back to the brain which helps to clear your mind and enable you to function properly. Do it four times. Start now: one – two – three – four...

- **Moving around**. Get up and stretch, make a cup of tea, go and wash your hands, pop outside on an errand or just to look at the weather.

With all these actions, movement is the crucial bit – it's a miniature form of fight and flight. Shifting the focus of your mind from what is 'threatening' gives you mental relief and consequently some physical reprieve from your system's 'battle stations'. Once your body begins to calm down, the stomach muscles relax, the digestive system starts working and the heartbeat slows, so you feel less tense. This, together with the fact that the brain is getting more oxygen, will help you think rationally.

Once you have started to think clearly, you will gain perspective and find that what was stressing you may not now seem so stressful.

Improving Your Work Surroundings

Think about the way you work and whether it is increasing your stress, or whether stress is dictating the way you work. There are a number of practical things you can do to improve your situation, such as:

- **Changing your working area**. If your working conditions are dreary, consider Feng Shui, the oriental system of laying out your belongings to encourage a feeling of congruity, by placing plants appropriately, removing mess, and creating a little corner of harmony. If you haven't got a view from a window, hang up a picture or a poster (even a post-card), of a scene with a perspective, because your eyes are best at rest when looking at infinity.

- **Having a good clear out**. If you seem to lose a piece of paper the moment you put it down, sort and get rid of the clutter. If files have not been used lately, archive them; if they are in current use, weed out what is unnecessary to keep. The very act of throwing things away is cathartic. When things are no longer in a muddle, your mind will follow suit.

- **Getting organized**. If you keep track of deadlines (on a wall chart or in your diary), this will help to eliminate the sense of helplessness which happens when you feel you are not in control.

- **Fixing things**. If you have equipment that does not do what it should, get it repaired or renewed. Fixing the photocopying machine that keeps getting jammed, and the shelf that wobbles, or buying a new filing cabinet, will make you feel you have achieved something concrete, especially when you next come to use it.

These are all simple remedies, but none of them are trivial. It is surprising how being able to find something quickly, or working with equipment that functions, or looking at something restful can reduce a large amount of the stress inherent in your working environment.

Relaxing

Developing the ability to relax is about actively engaging your parasympathetic nervous system (the one which restores energy). Watching television is one way to do this, and an even better way is the deliberate unwinding of mental and physical tension when you are completely at rest. So:

- Read a book – a thriller, 19th-century classic, biography, traveller's tale – anything which transports you from the stresses and strains of your daily life into one which is far removed from yours.

- Play a tape before you go to sleep of something soothing which makes you feel serene.

- Before you drift off, tense then relax the separate parts of your body: first your feet, then your legs, abdomen/torso, hands, arms, neck, shoulders, and finally your face. This releases all the tension bound up in the muscles and induces a state of physical tranquillity.

In addition to your own efforts, treatments provided by professionals can further the process of helping you to relax and feel better in yourself. For example:

- Aromatherapy which involves massage with fragrant oils that relieve tension.

- Deep-muscle massage which comprises kneading the body to promote better circulation, suppleness and ultimately relaxation.

- Reflexology which entails massage of the soles of the feet which, because they connect with other parts of the body, assist in relaxing it.

Engaging in methods of relaxation by yourself or putting yourself into skilled hands to reduce tension helps you become calm and produces a sense of well-being which gives you renewed energy to tackle your sources of stress.

Summary: Antidotes to Stress

Reducing stress means regularly lowering your stress levels so that they do not get out of hand.

This need not be a lone effort. You can enlist the help of others to help you relax and feel better, but best of all you can establish a programme of your own to ease your mind and body.

Improving your working environment means that you will be able to find that vital piece of paper without getting furious or frustrated. Having something peaceful to look at provides you with the opportunity to day-dream for a few moments so that you can return to your work invigorated. Deliberately relaxing your mind and body before you sleep lessens the tensions that have accumulated during the day.

Once you have seen the good effects of short-term remedies, it will encourage you to develop more permanent ways of reducing stress.

Questions to Ask Yourself

Think about ways of reducing stress and answer the following questions:

- Am I resolved to do something about my stress levels straight away?

- Am I prepared to try simple physical movement to reduce tension?

- Am I determined to improve my working methods and my surroundings?

- Am I motivated to organize myself better?

- Do I realize that working with non-functioning equipment causes stress?

- Do I appreciate that deliberately relaxing my mind and muscles before sleeping will lessen the tensions that have accumulated during the day.

You Will Be Doing Better If...

★ You understand that doing something to reduce stress levels is better than doing nothing.

★ You try the 'instant' remedies right away.

★ You are encouraged to do something to improve the surroundings in which you work.

★ You realize that having equipment in proper working order is a big help in reducing stress.

★ You understand the importance of physical movement to lessen feelings of tension and stress.

★ You appreciate that learning to relax will lower your stress levels.

5. Reducing Stress (Permanently)

To help yourself manage stress in a permanent way, take a look at your lifestyle and your own experience, and use your findings to develop long-term strategies for reducing stress.

Learning Healthy Habits

Consider the life you are leading and whether it is contributing to your stress, or whether stress itself is affecting your life. For instance, living for your work means you have only the work to focus on and, if it is not going well, your stress has no possibility of being relieved. To help defuse stress, you need to ensure you are not compounding bad habits induced by stress. You do this by:

- **Keeping to regular sleeping hours**. It may be that stress-induced fatigue is being exacerbated by a lack of sleep. The simple solution is an adequate amount. Late nights or early starts may have become routine and be depleting your energies. Break the old pattern by having one exceedingly late night and then start as you mean to go on by establishing a new pattern of 7-8 hours of sleep (using pre-sleep relaxation techniques) which will provide the means for the body to rest and recoup.

- **Eating healthy food**. Stressful eating of snatched snacks only leads to more stress. The quick boost they give is followed by you being left hungrier than before. The recipe is to take 10 minutes to sit down and eat (not a packet of crisps, but a salad or tuna sandwich), preferably away from your work. Give your body a chance to digest the food and absorb the nourishment it requires to perform well.

- **Drinking in moderation**. A little alcohol can help you relax and unwind. Too much, and it can act as the fuel to turn stress into anxiety and depression.

- **Fostering personal interests**. Being engrossed by something other than work stimulates your mind. You recharge your batteries and, when returning to work, can often find answers to things that have been worrying and stressing you.

- **Socializing, or not**. If you are an out-going person, fraternizing with people, expressing opinions and exchanging ideas can have a palliative effect. It puts stress on hold, and problems into perspective. And if you are a more inward-looking individual, taking a break from the hurly-burly by spending time quietly enjoying your own company can restore your composure. The appropriate strategy will allow your energy levels to revive which causes you to feel rejuvenated and more able to cope with stress.

Changing the bad habits caused by stress gives you the feeling that it is you who is running your life – and this is no illusion because, in fact, it is.

Taking Proper Exercise

However much the mere thought of exercise makes you feel you want to lie down, it is a guaranteed way to reduce stress. Lethargy breeds lethargy. Taking exercise makes you feel energetic because it helps your body to rid itself of harmful stress-related hormones. Exercise assists in the production of endorphins which give you a sense of well-being. You may find it difficult to believe, but once you begin to exercise you will become invigorated by it. Being 'on the go' all the time is not proper exercise. It has to be the running, cycling, stretching kind to have the right result.

If part of your reluctance towards exercise is a feeling of wasting time, you can use a personal stereo with tapes to provide mental stimulus at the same time and thus kill two birds with one stone.

Pick a form of exercise which suits you: this lessens the chance of your giving it up. Choose from:

● Walking briskly for 20 minutes each day. Apart from the good it will do, you will take in details of surroundings which you would never see from a bus, train or car.

- Digging out your old bicycle or acquiring one – and enjoying the exhilaration of travelling under your own steam.

- Buying an exercise video. You can do a work-out when it suits you and you need not feel self-conscious.

- Joining a sports club for aerobics, swimming or a physical training programme.

Exercise may initially seem an unattractive course of action but you need to realize it is essential to your well-being. If a hairy mammoth came at you, you would engage in exercise without a second thought. Think of everyday stress as your hairy mammoth.

Using Your Experience

Now, think about your own experience and what it can teach you. As the proverb goes: 'If you always do what you have always done, you will always get what you always got.' If you are stressed, learning new things is more difficult so you tend to carry on in the same old way. Try to apply what you already know by:

- **Recognizing your limits**. You know from painful experience what can and cannot be done, so setting realistic limits will make things look a lot more tangible and achievable.

- **Facing up to change**. You know when methods are cumbersome or obsolete, and that however tedious the process, changing them will make life easier.

- **Saying no**. You are usually aware when you might be taking on too much, so refusing to do something which you know will cause you stress is a sensible course of action – however hard others try to persuade you otherwise.

- **Accepting your shortcomings**. You know there is no such thing as being perfect, so recognizing that there are some areas where you have shortcomings and admitting to them means a lot less strain.

- **Avoiding certain people**. You know which people upset you, so making sure that you see them less will ensure they are able to upset you less.

- **Sizing up a situation**. Your experience will tell you if a certain course of action is likely to be stressful, so trusting your instincts as to whether or not to get involved may save you a lot of heartache.

- **Allowing time**. You know the feeling of panic caused by nearly missing a train or only just making a deadline. Allowing time to buy a newspaper at the station rather than leaping into a moving carriage, and getting ahead of yourself instead of leaving things till the last minute, is infinitely less stressful.

continuously under pressure from them means that you will be constantly lessening the pressure, and therefore lessening your stress.

Summary: Achieving a Balance

If you can make sure that there is a balance between your work and personal interests, as well as living a healthy life, you can alleviate much of the stress you may be experiencing.

Stress does not arrive on its own – it has a history – so when facing a new situation you can draw on your existing experience and use it to good effect.

Eating proper food, taking energetic exercise on a regular basis, and developing strategies for coping with worry will have an appreciable effect on your stress levels.

All these measures provide you with practical ways of reducing stress on a permanent basis.

Questions to Ask Yourself

Think about how you might reduce stress permanently and answer the following questions:

- Have I identified any bad habits which I need to change?

- Am I determined to take proper exercise now I know how important it is?

- Do I recognize that my own experience can help me to manage my stress?

- Do I realize that I can develop a methodical way to cope with my worries?

- Do I appreciate that standing back from my worries makes it easier to identify the real issue?

- Do I now understand that there are long-lasting strategies for combating stress?

You Will Be Doing Better If...

★ You resolve to change those habits which are preventing you from living a healthy life.

★ You choose a form of physical exercise which most suits you, and keep doing it.

★ You use your experience to prevent yourself from becoming embroiled in predictably stressful situations.

★ You develop a constructive approach to coping with your worries.

★ You shelve any worry that you can do nothing about at this moment.

★ You determine to keep practising stress-reducing methods so that they become part of your life.

6. Adopting a Positive Approach

Understanding stress is one thing, and learning how to handle it is another. But knowing what to do does not mean you will do it unless your feelings go hand in glove with your actions. Unfortunately, it is usually very difficult to adopt a positive approach when you are stressed. Not only do things tend to get out of focus, but negative thoughts predominate.

It is therefore a good idea periodically to re-establish a positive view of yourself and your values.

Verifying the Good

To regenerate positive feelings, you need to carry out an audit on yourself. By doing so, it is possible to confirm your attributes and verify the good things about your life. The vital areas involve:

- **Your goals**. Remind yourself of your original goals. You are likely to find that you are still on track and heading in your chosen direction. By reaffirming your aims, you renew your sense of purpose.

- **Your achievements**. Trace your achievements by considering what you have done and what you are proud of. You will be impressed by what you have achieved. The recognition of what you have already accomplished should encourage you to believe that you can do so again.

- **Your Expectations**. Check your standards against those of others. You will probably find that what you expect of yourself and your own performance is a great deal more than that which other people expect of themselves. In comparison your standards may well be way above average.

- **Your strengths**. Assess yourself in terms of what you are good at. You are likely to be better at more things than you think. By appreciating your strengths, you will gain in self-confidence.

The result of this personal audit is usually far more positive than you expect and will provide considerable encouragement.

Adjusting Your Perceptions

Experiments have been undertaken where people were given an injection of adrenaline, the major stress hormone. This caused them to feel the usual physiological reactions (quickening heartbeat, etc.), but as there was nothing to be worried about, no psychological reactions (dread, fear, apprehension) were experienced.

This proves that it is when people perceive themselves to be under pressure that stress results: it is their state of mind which causes the physiological and emotional reactions.

Unfortunately, the instinctive thing is to respond to negative feelings without realizing that it is the underlying thoughts which have provoked the response in the first place. So, for example, when collaborating with a difficult colleague, if you **think** "This person is impossible to work with" or "Whatever I do, it's never right for X" you will **feel** antagonistic so your **response** is likely to be an aggressive one.

The key to preventing hostile feelings from developing is to change the way you think (known as **cognitive processes**). When thoughts are positive, feelings tend to follow suit and lead to responses which are more likely to prevent stress being experienced.

With the difficult colleague, you would therefore:

1. **Think**: "X is very good on the technical side of the job, even if he is short-tempered." This enables you to...

2. **Feel** neutral towards him, which in turn leads you to...

3. **Respond** is a very focussed way by getting the task done and not engaging in chit-chat.

By making an effort to control your initial thoughts, you can prevent adverse emotions from arising. And at the end of the task, you will be surprised by how much you were able to achieve without becoming upset or irritated. This may even result in your considering that working with 'X' was not so bad after all.

If you do not view a situation as 'fearful', you do not flick the mental switch which prepares your body for the fight or flight response and floods it with feelings of apprehension. As a result, stress is kept at bay.

Embracing the Locus of Control

People who believe that they are in command of their own actions perceive their lives to be less stressful than those who think the outside world is in charge. This concept is called the 'locus of control'.

If you have an internal 'locus of control' you believe that you are master of what happens to you. If, on the other hand, you have an external locus, you believe that your life is controlled by exterior forces. Though neither view is totally realistic, you need to realize that you can have a big hand in your destiny and that it is this which determines your core attitudes to coping with stress.

So if you can convince yourself that you control your circumstances, you are far less likely to succumb to the pressures felt by those who believe that circumstances are controlling them.

The more you remind yourself that it is within you to control what happens to you, the less you feel like a leaf being tossed about by a storm. Thinking of yourself as being at the mercy of the elements induces stress, whereas thinking of yourself as always being able to do something about anything that happens reduces stress.

Summary: Handling Stress

When you adopt a positive approach to your life and work, you change how you view yourself and how you view stressful situations.

By refusing to let negative thoughts dictate how you are going to feel, and therefore function, you will find yourself with the power to take charge of your life and the confidence to do so.

It is important to appreciate that you have far more choice over the way you feel than you realize.

Believing that you have control and are in charge of events goes a long way to ensuring that you are effective in handling stress.

Questions to Ask Yourself

Think about how you view stress and answer the following questions:

- Have I reminded myself recently of my overall goals?

- Have I recently considered my achievements and evaluated them?

- Do I recognize that I probably perform better than a great many others?

- Do I appreciate the extent of my personal strengths?

- Do I understand that a negative state of mind produces negative reactions which activate stress?

- Do I accept that positive thoughts lead to positive behaviour which makes many situations far less stressful?

- Do I believe that I am in control of my fate?

You Will Be Doing Better If...

★ You keep your goals in mind and review them regularly.

★ You acknowledge your achievements.

★ You reassure yourself that you are doing as well, if not better, than other people.

★ You remind yourself from time to time of your personal strengths.

★ You make an effort to change negative thoughts into positive ones.

★ You are convinced that it is you, and only you, who controls what happens to you.

★ You know that by adopting a positive approach you will handle stress better.

Check List for Handling Stress

Should you find that your efforts to handle stress are not working as well you expected, consider whether this is because you have failed to take account of one or more of the following aspects:

Understanding Stress

If you feel tetchier and more miserable than usual, you may not have realized that this is the result of stress. You may be finding it less easy to think straight or react rationally because your body thinks it is under siege and has prepared itself for battle. This means that you are all geared up to attack or to cut and run, but usually you can do neither. Understanding that there are both physical and mental forces at play can help to explain why you are feeling under pressure.

Pinpointing Stressors

If you are blaming yourself for not coping with difficulties, it may be that you have skipped the process of pinpointing where your stress is coming from. Perhaps the need to cope with changing circumstances is at the root of your stress. Maybe you are pushing yourself too hard. Or it could be that you have not made allowances for the sheer number of worries and problems you have to cope with all at once.

Reducing Stress (Instantly)

Should bouts of tension and anxiety be disrupting your work, it is possible that you are forgetting to try simple stress-busting techniques. Or you may not be properly organized so you cannot find things easily. Perhaps you have no calming vista to look at when you need a mental escape from your surroundings. Or you may not be remembering to relax your muscles before you go to sleep.

Reducing Stress (Permanently)

If your stress continues to be a persistent presence, you may not have got round to enacting the major stress-alleviating formulas. Perhaps you tried them but did not persevere. You may not be taking sufficient exercise to rid your body of unused adrenaline. Or you may even have slipped back into unhealthy habits.

Your Approach to Stress

If you feel events are taking you over, it may be you do not yet accept that it is you who are in charge of your stress. By remembering that it is the way you perceive situations and interpret them that sets up a stress spiral, you can break the sequence. But, above all, it is only when you truly believe that taking a positive approach to stress will make all the difference that you will be able to handle it successfully.

The Benefits of Handling Stress

Stress is an everyday part of life but once you understand its nature and have identified its causes, you can take steps to counteract it.

Being able to handle stress has wide-ranging benefits:

- You feel more energetic and enthusiastic about your life and work.

- You can think more clearly and logically.

- You are less likely to get exhausted or upset.

- You look and feel better.

- You are more productive and often more creative.

- You are more able to keep yourself calm and regenerate your inner reserves.

- You know there is always something that you can do to help yourself to reduce stress.

Knowing that you can control your stress and that it need not control you is a great relief.

However stressed you are, once you start practising stress-reducing techniques, you will feel the beneficial effects on your life and performance. All it needs is the will to begin.

Glossary

Here are some definitions in relation to Stress.

Anxiety – A lurking dread that something nasty is about to happen.

Balance – A state of equilibrium which is the antidote to stress.

Burnout – An extreme state of mental and physical exhaustion induced by stress. All ash, no spark.

Cognitive Processes – The initial thoughts which influence feelings which in turn influence behaviour. It's all in the mind.

Coping – Being able to keep up with demands.

Depression – The feeling of being in a dark tunnel with no light, and no end in sight.

Intrinsic Drivers – Internal compulsions which determine the way you do things. Fine, until they get out of hand.

Exercise – Deliberate exertion. The single most effective way of reducing stress.

Fight/Flight – Primitive reactions to fear which remain the body's response to threat, real or imagined.

Hypothalamus – The 'stress centre' in the brain which regulates the body's balance.

Locus of Control – The degree to which people believe they are masters of their own fate.

Parasympathetic System – The body's equivalent of a cup of hot tea and a blanket.

Negative strategies – Ineffective methods for coping with stress which result in your doing all the wrong things.

Positive attitude – Thinking good things about your life and yourself.

Stress – Mental and physical pressure resulting in an inability to cope, and made worse by that inability.

Stressor – Anything which causes you stress – from queues to corrupt computers.

Sympathetic System – The body's equivalent of a regiment of artillery, fired up and ready for action.

The Author

Kate Keenan is a Chartered Occupational Psychologist with degrees in affiliated subjects (B.Sc., M.Phil.) and a number of qualifications in others.

She founded Keenan Research, an industrial psychology consultancy, in 1978. The work of the consultancy is fundamentally concerned with helping people to achieve their potential and make a better job of their management.

By devising work programmes for companies she enables them to target and remedy their managerial problems – from personnel selection and individual assessment to team building and attitude surveys. She believes in giving priority to training the managers to institute their own programmes, so that their company resources are developed and expanded.

Being an expert in analysing the causes of stress means that she is rather better at helping others to reduce their stress than getting to grips with her own. However, writing this book has provoked a long over-due impetus to practice what she preaches – beginning with relaxing her shoulders and taking four deep breaths.

THE MANAGEMENT GUIDES

	Book £2.99	Tape £4.99
Asserting Yourself	☐	
Communicating*	☐	☐
Delegating*	☐	☐
Handling Stress	☐	
Making Time*	☐	☐
Managing*	☐	☐
Managing Yourself*	☐	☐
Motivating*	☐	☐
Negotiating*	☐	☐
Planning*	☐	☐
Running Meetings*	☐	☐
Selecting People*	☐	☐
Solving Problems*	☐	☐
Understanding Behaviour*	☐	☐

Just tick the titles you require and send a cheque or postal order for the value of the book to: B.B.C.S., P.O. Box 941, Hull HU1 3VQ (24 hour Telephone Credit Card Line: 01482 224626). Add for postage & packing (in the UK) £1.00 for the first book & 50p for each extra book up to a maximum of £2.50. Overseas (& Eire) Orders: £2.00 for the first book, £1.00 for the second & 50p for each additional book.

*These books are also available on audio tape. Telephone 0800 435 067, or send a cheque or postal order for the value of the tape to: Quantum Leap Group, P.O. Box 510, Milton Keynes MK8 0ZT, and add for postage & packing the same amount as specified for book postage above.